Monster of the Movies

Beauty and the Beast

Monster of the Movies

David Annan

Bounty Books

Copyright © MCMLXXV by
Lorrimer Publishing Ltd.
Library of Congress Catalog Number: 74–29103
All rights reserved
This edition is published by Bounty Books
a division of Crown Publishers Inc.
by arrangement with Lorrimer Publishing Ltd

ISBN 0–517–521563

Printed in Great Britain by
Hazell Watson and Viney Ltd, Aylesbury, Bucks

Contents

Acknowledgements

We wish to give our thanks in the preparation of this book to Jonathan Swift, Edgar Allan Poe, Charles Darwin, Rudyard Kipling, Willis O'Brien, Merian C. Cooper, Ernest Schoedsack, Pierre Boulle, Arthur Jacobs, *Midi-Minuit Fantastique* No. 3, *Focus on Film* No. 16, RKO Pictures, 20th Century-Fox, Paramount, MGM, Columbia, Warner Brothers, United Artists, Allied Artists, Anglo-Amalgamated, First National, Universal, Anglo-EMI, Rank, British Lion, Hammer Films, the British Film Institute, the Cinema Bookshop, Al Reuter, the Museum of Modern Art and many others who have made the ape loom large in our dreams.

DESCENT OF APE

We are all the kin of King Kong. The monkey is the ancestor of man, just as the gorilla is the forerunner of the giant. In our subconscious, we dream dimly of our primaeval past when we lived hairy in the trees and battled the monsters of the swamps. King Kong is the Goliath of our prehistory. His combats and love and death are mightier and more ancient than those of Hercules or Thor, for they derive from the time millions of years ago, when men were beasts struggling slowly towards the fire in the cave.

The recent discoveries of fossils by the Leakeys in East Africa have shown that different types of ape evolved into at least four species of humanoid beings, one of which became man. After Charles Darwin's discovery of evolution

Australopithecus, one of the half-way points between apes and men, used to hunt in prehistoric Africa.

more than a hundred years ago, which caused the largest split between scientists and clergymen since the days of Galileo, many writers have tried to discover the point at which the soul actually entered the ape: when monkey could actually be called man. Perhaps William Golding's novel *The Inheritors* and Vercors' *Les Animaux Dénaturés* are the two most searching inquiries into the common origins of apes and human beings. Nevertheless, the film of *King Kong* remains the most moving and haunting suggestion of the terrible bond between all creatures that have evolved from the little living cells that once walked on legs out of the original seas.

All ancient countries, which have known of the existence of apes, have feared them and sometimes worshipped them. The Chinese had a Monkey-God who was vindictive, tricky and powerful. Some of the forest tribes of Africa and Central America thought the ape divine and wore monkey-skins and masks in their ceremonial dances to make themselves strong. In medieval Europe, the existence of giant apes was known and they joined the popular fears of strange monsters which peopled the unknown world. Rudyard Kipling turned this terror into a tale in *Puck of Pook's Hill*, where he made the Vikings sail to Africa and battle against creatures which they called Devils – and which we know to be gorillas.

Pat Suzuki plays Tropazia, the human ape in Gordon Douglas's *Skullduggery* (1970), based on Vercors' novel.

An illustration by R. Millar from the 1906 edition of *Puck of Pook's Hill*.

Yet giant apes were largely unknown in Europe until the spread of zoological gardens after the eighteenth century. The literary inventor of the idea of King Kong seems to be that expert in scaling people up and down, Jonathan Swift. Although he borrowed the idea of giants from Rabelais, his vision of the monkey which stole Gulliver on his travels to Brobdingnag was all his own.

In Swift's masterpiece, the tiny Lemuel Gulliver finds himself among a race of human giants and is locked up in his doll's house, rather like the hero of the later film *The Incredible Shrinking Man*. Another pet of the giants of Brobdingnag, a monkey as large as themselves, decides to peep into Gulliver's doll's house for pleasure and curiosity. The episode continues:

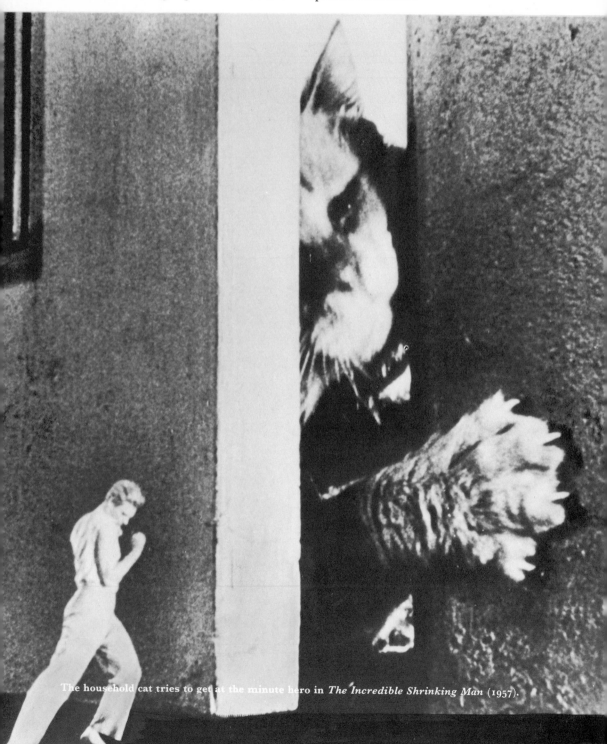

The household cat tries to get at the minute hero in *The Incredible Shrinking Man* (1957).

I retreated to the farther Corner of my Room, or Box; but the Monkey looking in at every Side, put me into such a Fright, that I wanted Presence of Mind to conceal myself under the Bed, as I might easily have done. After some time spent in peeping, grinning, and chattering, he at last espied me; and reaching one of his Paws in at the Door, as a Cat does when she plays with a Mouse, although I often shifted Place to avoid him; he at length seized the Lappet of my Coat . . . and dragged me out.

He took me up in his right Fore-foot, and held me as a Nurse doth a child she is going to suckle; just as I have seen the same Sort of Creature do with a Kitten in Europe; and when I offered to struggle, he squeezed me so hard, that I thought it more prudent to submit. I have good Reason to believe that he took me for a young one of his own Species, by his often stroking my Face very gently with his other Paw. In these Diversions he was interrupted by a Noise at the Closet Door, as if some Body were opening it; whereupon he suddenly leaped up to the Window at which he had come in, and thence upon the Leads and Gutters, walking upon three Legs, and holding me in the fourth, till he clambered up to a Roof that was next to ours.

That Quarter of the Palace was all in an Uproar; the Servants ran for Ladders; the Monkey was seen by Hundreds in the Court, sitting upon the Ridge of a Building, holding me like a Baby in one of his Fore-Paws, and feeding me with the other, by cramming into my Mouth some Victuals he had squeezed out of the Bag on one Side of his Chaps, and patting me when I would not eat; whereat many of the Rabble below could not forebear laughing; neither do I think they justly ought to be blamed; for without Question, the Sight was ridiculous enough to every Body but myself. Some of the People threw up Stones, hoping to drive the Monkey down; but this was strictly forbidden, or else very probably my Brains had been dashed out.

The Ladders were now applied, and mounted by several Men; which the Monkey observing, and finding himself almost encompassed; not being able to make Speed enough with his three Legs, let me drop on a Ridge-Tile, and made his Escape. Here I sat for some time five Hundred Yards from the Ground, expecting every Moment to be blown down by the Wind, or to fall by my own Giddiness, and come tumbling over and over from the Ridge to the Eaves. But an Honest Lad . . . climbed up, and putting me into his Breeches Pocket, brought me down safe . . .

The Monkey was killed, and an Order made that no such Animal should be kept about the Palace.

The monkey tries to seize the tiny Lemuel in Job's illustration for *Gulliver's Travels* in a French edition of 1900.

King Kong takes Fay Wray up to the top of a skyscraper in this drawing from the RKO Press Book of 1933.

The monkey takes Lemuel to the rooftops in an Italian edition of *Gulliver's Travels*.

The giant monkey fondles Lemuel Gulliver in Grandville's drawing about 1850.

The honest Mate climbs to the rescue of the abandoned girl on the top of the Empire State Building in *King Kong*.

14

Aubrey Beardsley's ape carries off the dead girl to stuff her up the chimney.

Jonathan Swift's satire on Gulliver and the giant monkey seemed more real when the explorers returned from Africa and the East Indies in the eighteenth and nineteenth centuries, bringing reports of giant apes, gorillas and orang-outangs. One Scots lawyer, Lord Monboddo, was ridiculed when he tried to prove in 1774 that the orang-outang was of the same species as human beings. Its very name, Monboddo said, meant a wild man. It walked erect; the females were modest and could cry. The orang-outang had a human intelligence, was kind and friendly, lived in huts and fought with a stick 'which no animal, merely brute, is known to do.' In fact, Monboddo

Arthur Rackham's orang-outang slashes off the mother's head with a razor.

The orang-outang attacks its master, Bela Lugosi, in the 1931 version.

thought that the East Indian apes were merely hairy men. But nobody believed him at the time.

That mid-Victorian master of the macabre, Edgar Allan Poe, used the same travellers' tales in his mystery, *The Murders in the Rue Morgue*. In the story, a pair of brutal murders in Paris are discovered to be the crime of an orang-outang, brought by a sailor from Borneo, only to escape with his master's razor. Both Aubrey Beardsley and Arthur Rackham illustrated the story and four film versions of it were made. Even Bela Lugosi could not save the first one. Somehow, the drawings of the murderous ape are more horrifying than the caperings of the man dressed as an orang-outang on the screen. And neither were as fearful as the restrained words of Edgar Allan Poe describing the outrage:

The orang-outang threatens the maiden in the film of *Murders in the Rue Morgue* (1931).

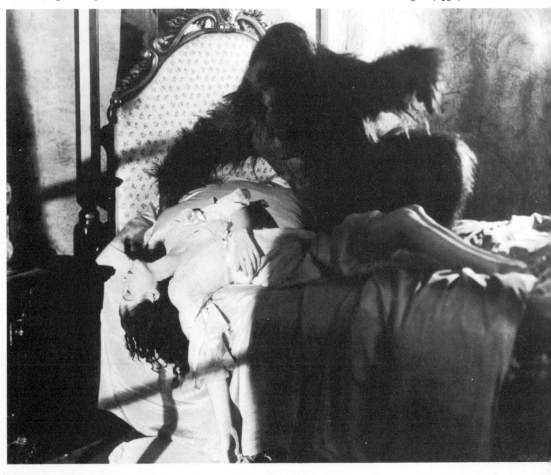

As the sailor looked in, the gigantic animal had seized Madame L'Espanaye by the hair (which was loose, as she had been combing it), and was flourishing the razor about her face, in imitation of the motions of a barber. The daughter lay prostrate and motionless; she had swooned. The screams and struggles of the old lady (during which the hair was torn from her head) had the effect of changing the probably pacific purposes of the Orang-Outang into those of wrath. With one determined sweep of its muscular arm it nearly severed her head from her body. The sight of blood inflamed its anger into frenzy. Gnashing its teeth, and flashing fire from its eyes, it flew upon the body of the girl, and imbedded its fearful talons in her throat, retaining its grasp until she expired. Its wandering and wild glances fell at this moment upon the head of the bed, over which the face of its master, rigid with horror, was just discernible. The fury of the beast, who no doubt bore still in mind the dreaded whip, was instantly converted into fear. Conscious of having deserved punishment, it seemed desirous of concealing its bloody deeds, and skipped about the chamber in an agony of nervous agitation; throwing down and breaking the

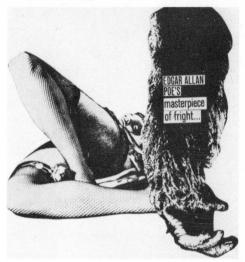

The vile paw menaces the fallen girl in the American International remake of *Murders in the Rue Morgue.*

furniture as it moved, and dragging the bed from the bedstead. In conclusion, it seized first the corpse of the daughter, and thrust it up the chimney, as it was found; then that of the old lady, which it immediately hurled through the window headlong . . . There lay the corpse of the old lady, with her throat so entirely cut that, upon attempt to raise her, the head fell off . . .

A teaser from the pressbook of the 1945 remake of Poe's story excites the audience with the puzzle – savage ape or murdering man?

It mauls...it rips...it vanishes! A mammoth monstrous man-or-phantom rising out of the depths beneath the city!

So Swift and Poe developed the opposite themes that were later to be brought together in *King Kong*. As in Swift's story, the giant ape Kong is gentle with his beloved captive, seizes her through a window, carries her off to a high roof, abandons her there and is killed for his act of love. But as in Poe's story, Kong is also a ravening beast who eats men alive, destroys their homes, bringing horror to the city and leaving its gutters running with blood. The split nature of Kong, the gentle and the terrible, the amorous and the horrendous, are expressed in these two earlier versions of the theme.

Yet the real genesis of the Kong legend lies in Charles Darwin's theory of evolution. His discovery that men had evolved from an ape-like primate was popularised and distorted until it became part of mass myth. One contemporary caricature of 1871 showed Darwin himself as a monkey. In fact, Darwin presumed a common ancestor millions of years ago; but his researches allowed for popular writers to put *human* traits into the giant apes biologically, as Swift had done satirically into Gulliver's monkey.

Charles Darwin drawn as an ape, although he never suggested that man was similar to any simian now known.

Adam and Eve in the Garden of Eden. An engraving by Dürer (1504), where the evil is the serpent, not the ape. Also a drawing by Gustave Doré (left).

The fight of the Christian churches against the theory of evolution, their effort to keep Adam and Eve in the Garden of Eden and the gorillas and the chimpanzees outside, resulted in a world-wide interest in monkeys and their behaviour, which has only grown with the years. If *King Kong* was the

The wise ape in *Planet of the Apes,* showing a remarkable resemblance to Darwin. This modern cycle of films relies on the popular belief that Darwin found a common ground between men and monkeys, and that literate apes might evolve out of men in the future.

first film to exploit this global interest, it was the heir of Rudyard Kipling, Rider Haggard and Edgar Rice Burroughs, just as it was the ancestor of that most recent success, *The Naked Ape*, which is devoted to showing how human behaviour parallels that of monkeys. Fantasy-writers, film-makers and popular biologists have mined gold from Darwin's discovery and from mass dreams.

In Rudyard Kipling's successful Jungle Books, the wild boy Mowgli is brought up by the Wolf Pack, while the Monkey People of the high branches are chattering, vindictive and despised. Likewise, the baboons in Rider Haggard's *Allan's Wife*. Led by the ape-woman Hendrika (a white girl brought up by them), the baboons steal a woman, Stella, and a little girl, who have to be rescued from a fate worse than death at their paws. Hints of bestiality and sexuality appear in Haggard's text as they do in the later *King Kong*, but Edwardian decencies keep the words veiled. Stella's dress is nearly torn off by the baboons, but just enough remains on to keep her respectable. The baboons try to molest her, but are fought off by the ape-woman Hendrika, who loves her captive because Stella had once rescued her from the baboons, although she has now returned to them. Eventually, Allan Quatermain, the mighty hunter, exterminates the baboons with his elephant gun, and rescues his wife Stella and the

Balaoo in the first full-length ape-man film.

child. But Stella dies and Quatermain later finds the dying Hendrika wailing on his wife's grave. She moans for her split nature, half-human, half-ape. 'I killed her!' the dying woman falters, 'And I loved her . . . I became a brute again and dragged her to the brutes, and now once more I am a woman, and she is dead, and I killed her – because I loved her so. I killed her who saved me from the brutes.' Saying this, Hendrika dies, unable like the later Kong to reconcile her human love of Stella with her bestial jealousy and ferocity.

The original films on monkeys made use of their evil qualities. Two shorts were made in 1908 in France. In the first, *The Doctor's Experiment*, patients were injected with simian serum and began to gibber. In the second, *The Monkey Man*, a simian brain was transplanted into a human skull. In both films, man became ape. From a combination of these plots a feature film was made by Eclair in 1913 called *Balaoo the Demon Baboon*. It was imitated in the early days of Hollywood by three features in 1927, exploiting the publicity given to the 'monkey trial' of a teacher, who had dared to preach the evolution theory in a biblical Southern state. In *The Gorilla* of 1927, Walter Pidgeon actually had to perform in an ape-suit, although he successfully played in the flesh and the shadow of the ape in the remake three years later. *The Wizard* also featured a fiend-faced ape as a demon villain. *The Monkey Talks*, however, had a dwarf French actor wearing a chimpanzee suit and feeling up a circus girl, whom he later saved from the assaults of a real ape.

Above and Centre: Walter Pidgeon plays the gorilla in the skin . . . and outside it, in these two versions of *The Gorilla* (1927 and 1930). Below: Jacques Lerner in the monkey suit tries to show his love for the circus girl.

The unconscious Tarzan is rescued by his devoted apes.

Yet Edgar Rice Burroughs' famous series of Tarzan books give the ape a fair name. The apes, which bring up the lost English lordling like Hendrika, are now good, and where they are occasionally evil, Tarzan fights them to the death. It is the African natives, indeed, who are held to be devilish, while the jungle animals as in Kipling are innocent in the wild. The success of the Tarzan stories as mass comics and escapist films, attest to a mass fantasy of returning to an unspoilt and uncivilised life in the virgin forest, where the last of the gorillas still are kings.

Cheeta, the friendly chimpanzee, cuddles up with Tarzan's girl, instead of kidnapping her.

As more and more came to be known of the last of the actual giant apes, so the sadness that is at the root of the story of King Kong came to be revealed. There are only some five thousand gorillas now left in the bamboo forests of the Congo. They are evolutionary failures. Their huge arms and chests are useless now because they no longer swing through the trees like Tarzan. They stay on the ground and build themselves nests there. Their legs are too short for getting about at speed. Their sexual drive is far from the loving lust of a King Kong.

Gorillas, indeed, are dying out from a lack of interest in copulation. They very rarely fight, being rather shy. One fight, which did take place in 1958 on the slopes of Mount Muhavura, lasted for twelve days and ended in the death of one of the male gorillas. But such Kong-like combats are rare. Gorillas seem to be caught in the melancholy knowledge of having lost their place in evolution and being forced to die. They are so lazy that they relieve themselves where they sleep, and fouling one's own nest is a sign of a species no longer interested in its survival. Yet, as Robert Ardrey once wrote, the tragic figure sloping through the cloudy forests of mysterious African volcanoes still clings to the treasure of his dominance, and he will clutch that most precious of animal possessions even to his species' grave.

King Kong, the greatest ape of them all, ready for battle. From a drawing by the master of special effects, Willis O'Brien.

King Kong, too, was mighty on his own ground and doomed by the gas-bombs and machine guns of civilisation. He could triumph over the prehistoric beasts of the swamp and the ptero-dactyls of the air, but the screaming half-naked New York floozie and the fighter-planes defeated him. He was the noble savage of the jungle faced with the treacheries of mechanics and cities. And so he is crucified in the exhibition hall and breaks free to protest in the only way he knows: through brute force and the rape of what he loves. His death is not to save mankind, but to deny its intrusion on his simple dominion and its exploitation of his gargantuan power.

The gigantic ape confronts civilisation in the persons of a mighty white hunter and a half-naked jungle girl. This original painting by O'Brien and Byron Crabbe persuaded Merian Cooper to proceed with them in the making of *King Kong*.

King Kong defends his love from the attack of a pterodactyl.

KING KONG
FAY WRAY
ROB'T ARMSTRONG
BRUCE CABOT
A PERSONALLY DIRECTED
MERIAN C·
COOPER
ERNEST B·
SCHOEDSACK
PRODUCTION
FROM THE STORY BY MERIAN C·COOPER and EDGAR
RKO RADIO PICTURES

King Kong is crucified by the showman, Carl Denham, for the audience in New York.

Another crucifixion scene by Grunëwald, about 1524.

The film of King Kong not only uses the myths of our primitive past and of our religion, but also exploits the fear and fantasy of the monster carrying away the sacrificial white maiden. The legends of Perseus rescuing Andromeda from the dragon became the titillations of a more sexually-conscious age, where the giant ape slowly strips the clothes off his love, then smells the female scent lingering on his finger. The giant ape also finally climbs with her to the top of the tallest erection in New York – a pinnacle of rape. The sexual symbolism of King Kong is as old as the first menhir set up in Neolithic times. The Empire State Building is merely a taller phallic stone.

Such is the descent of King Kong. He straddles our memories as he straddles our cities. He is the giant of our fantasies of power. He is the victim of our grovellings in love. He is the nightmare from the jungles of our

King Kong slowly strips Fay Wray, from a drawing by Willis O'Brien. Although these scenes were shot, they were cut from the final version.

primitive memories. He is the terror of our total destruction. He is the force of nature that men try to control and exploit, and cannot. King Kong is the voluptuous termination that threatens all our little lives.

Above: King Kong rages from the top of his skyscraper.

Left: The Celtic cross at Maen Achwyfan, about 1000 A.D. The Christians merely decorated the phallic stone shapes they found with the symbols of their religion.

KING KONG

FAY WRAY · ROBERT ARMSTRONG · BRUCE CABOT

A MERIAN C. COOPER ERNEST B. SCHOEDSACK PRODUCTION

STARTLING! STAGGERING! SENSATIONAL!

MAKING OF KONG

The idea of filming a giant ape came from Africa, where a Hollywood documentary film-maker, Merian C. Cooper, was shooting with Ernest B. Schoedsack some footage on wild life for Paramount's version of *The Four Feathers*. The year was 1929. Cooper became obsessed with the vision of a giant gorilla going berserk in a modern city. The ape would fight a giant lizard – some of these miniature dragons had just been discovered on the island of Komodo – and it would end by dying on the top of the Empire State Building. Cooper took the concept back with him to Hollywood, where his friend David O. Selznick had become the production chief of RKO Pictures. But he made no headway with the project, until he met the man who could actually make the monster ape, and within the studio.

The mighty ape rages against men. From an original drawing by Willis O'Brien.

That man was Willis O'Brien. He had invented the tricks of animating rubber-and-wire models for the old Edison Studios, and made one original, five-minute short film called *The Dinosaur and the Missing Link*, in which the prehistoric monster disposes of the primitive hairy man. O'Brien did well enough to venture on filming Conan Doyle's *The Lost World* as a full-length feature. By the use of glass shots, stop-frame filming, miniature sets, and his model monsters, which even seemed to breathe, O'Brien completed the feature. In it, Professor Challenger, played by Wallace Beery, accompanies the daughter of a lost explorer, played by

Right: Bull Montana plays the apeman or Missing Link in *The Lost World*.

Below: Two prehistoric monsters battle to the death in Willis O'Brien's *The Lost World* (1925).

The apeman is confused by the machines of modern times ... and he menaces the escape of the explorers from the prehistoric plateau.

Bessie Love, to the top of a plateau in South America where prehistoric creatures still battle to the death. The seeds of King Kong lie in this film: particularly in the battle of a Tyrannosaurus Rex with a Triceratops and the attacks of an ape-man, played by Bull Montana. The explorers also manage to bring back with them to London a Brontosaurus, which breaks loose in the docks and partially wrecks the city, before swimming down the Thames and out to sea.

These elements from the plot of *The Lost World*, plus the actual wizardry in animation of Willis O'Brien, were the catalyst which gave birth to Merian Cooper's concept of the giant gorilla. O'Brien had failed at setting up three other monster - against - man films: *Atlantis*, *Frankenstein* and *Creation*. In the last, however, he had shot some superb test footage of a sailor shooting a baby Triceratops and being pursued through the jungle by its enraged mother – a scene very similar to a later one in *King Kong*. When Cooper saw the

excellence of the footage, he decided to scrap the plot of *Creation* and to include O'Brien's ideas in his concept of the gargantuan ape. As Edgar Wallace was then working in Hollywood, the British mystery writer was hired to do a treatment of the script, but he died of pneumonia early in 1932. The script was completed by Cooper, James Creelman and Ruth Rose, who was married to Cooper's collaborator, Schoedsack. RKO Pictures, however, were not yet convinced enough of the potential of the film, so the shooting of only one reel was authorised as a test. O'Brien produced the marvellous scene where King Kong shakes some sailors from a log down into a chasm below, and then goes on to battle a Tyrannosaurus Rex. The reel was a huge success with the studio executives and *King Kong* was scheduled for full production.

Above: The prehistoric beast forces the sailors to fall to their death by uprooting a log bridge. From a drawing by Byron Crabbe, a collaborator with O'Brien.

Below: Edgar Wallace dreams of King Kong in this publicity montage.

The film took more than a year to shoot and cost two-thirds of a million dollars, a large budget for the times. While O'Brien's sketches and experience provided the working methods, his model-makers, the brothers Delgado, made the incredible monsters. These were usually sixteen to eighteen inches high, and constructed on steel skeletons covered with latex muscles and cotton, and finally enclosed in a skin of liquid latex. Back-projection and glass shots

King Kong battles to prove himself master of the primeval jungle. From a drawing by Willis O'Brien, and a still from the film.

allowed for human beings to appear in scale and size with these little monsters. But vast models of Kong's paw, foot, head and chest, as well as the claws of the pterodactyl that carries off Fay Wray, also had to be built. These could persuade the audience of the reality of the mice-large humans compared with the mighty monsters, particularly since some of the humans themselves were occasionally represented by miniature rubber dolls in the monster shots.

Nothing was omitted to add to the realism of the illusion. Birds seem to fly through the prehistoric jungles, water flows through Kong's cave. On the sound track, the Tyrannosaurus Rex's hiss was taken from a puma's scream combined with an air-compressor, while Kong's chest-beating roar was recorded by a microphone on a man's back, registering the thumps of a padded drumstick on his ribs. So slow was the process of animation, so meticulous the care of preparation, that a hard day's work did not yield more than half a minute of screen-time.

Left: The largest of the Kong models built in the studio.

The brothers Delgado construct the skeleton of a giant paw for King Kong.

Buzz Gibson animates the model of King Kong, as he climbs the side of the Empire State Building.

Carl Denham rescues Ann, played by Fay Wray, from the streets of New York, and persuades her to come with him on an unknown expedition.

The gate, which separates the native village from Kong's domain, was left over on the studio lot from the filming of the *King of Kings*.

Yet the genius of *King Kong* lies in the fact that the special effects do not overwhelm the story. The slow opening in New York during the depression is realistic enough to persuade an audience of the actuality of events. The transition from the familiar to the absurd is almost imperceptible. And, of course, the film is absurd. In a famous essay on *King Kong*, Jean Ferry listed the abnormalities of the plot: the taking out of the actress to film a documentary, the gate (left over from the shooting of *King of Kings*) which separates Kong from the native village, the ease with which Kong finds the girl in New York, and

the absolute ridiculousness of scale – at one point, Kong's paw is large enough to crush a train, at another time, only large enough to be a magic carpet for the screaming girl. But Jean Ferry also says that the abnormalities do not matter. For, despite the opening illusion of realism, *King Kong* is the dream of the monster who pursues us terrifyingly through the labyrinths of nightmare. We cannot escape. His size grows and recedes. He finds us wherever we hide. Kong is always there, ready to rage and kill. And yet we escape, as in a dream. Kong is the fear of inevitable revenge, the horror of the dead of night.

King Kong towers over New York, yet his paw is only large enough to hold Fay Wray.

Willis O'Brien's artwork increases the feeling of being trapped in a dream. As the critics of Kong in *Midi-Minuit Fantastique* point out, O'Brien's influences are the Gothic designs of Gustave Doré, the Böcklin painting of the 'Isle of the Dead', and the submarine caves of Max Ernst. In one sequence, King Kong draws up the escaping girl and her lover on a creeper, as mighty as the giant Antaeus putting down Vergil and Dante into Doré's version of the Inferno. Paul Eluard, the surrealist poet, once accepted the presidency of a film club with the words: 'I would like it, but will you be showing *King Kong* again?'

Yet before presenting the plot of the existing film, which haunts our imaginations, it is necessary to discover what was cut out by censor or distributor. The most exotic sequence, in which King Kong slowly peels the clothing off Fay Wray and then sniffs the female

Ruth Rose had herself been a strip-tease artist before becoming a scenarist on *King Kong*.

The giant Antaeus lowers Virgil and Dante into the Inferno in Doré's drawing.

Kong tries to pull up the escaping lovers on their convenient creeper.

The sailor about to be eaten. From the cut footage of *King Kong*.

Imitating the foot-crushing Kong, the Djinn's foot menaces *The Thief of Baghdad* (1939).

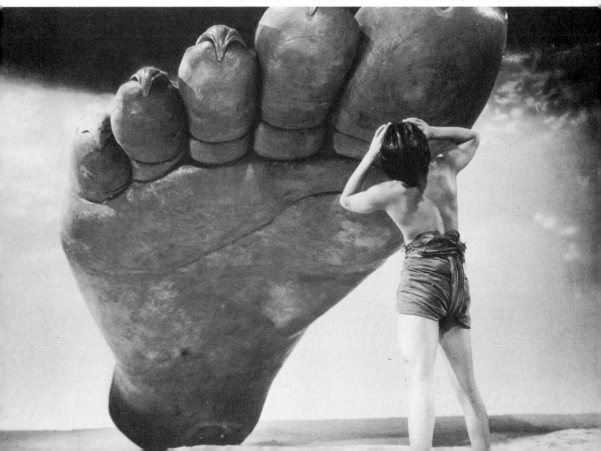

38

The man-eating
spiders were
filmed eating the
sailors.

scent on his finger, has been lopped
from most existing versions – too titilla-
ting, too phallic. Equally, certain
brutal sequences have been cut – the
Tyrannosaurus Rex eating a sailor,
King Kong eating a native in the
village and squashing a baby. Cut also
was the most casual and shocking
sequence of all (as indifferent a murder
as that of Frankenstein's monster throwing the child like a flower in the water

to drown), that of Kong reaching
through a skyscraper window to look
for his girl, taking out the wrong
woman, and discarding her down the
side of the hotel building. Missing, too,
was the sequence where the sailors,
shaken from the log by Kong, fall into a
ravine and are devoured by giant
lizards, man-eating plants and spiders.
Much of the eroticism and sadism has
been scissored from the work.

A contemporary cartoon of the story draws
Kong's paw shattering the hotel window,
before discarding the wrong girl down the
skyscraper.

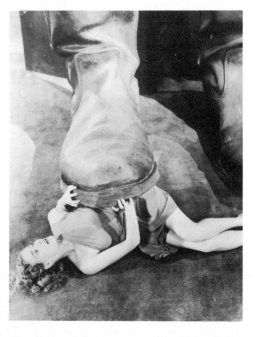

Dr. Cyclops' foot menaces his little victim
(1940).

Yet a film of extraordinary imagination remains. For Elliot Stein, not only the hidden depths of Freud and Jung are still conjured up, but also the world of Marx, where the starving actress in depression New York will accept a job at the risk of her life, merely to eat. The follies of a mad love – for how can the giant ape ever *sleep* with his screaming maiden? – the sexual symbolism of finger and paw and Empire State Building, the sadism of the combats, the masochism of the trials of the victim in white, all these elements make a film of obsessive power that has never been equalled, and haunts us always.

The sailors fall into the ravine. From O'Brien's drawing.

One of the publicity posters for the film.

King Kong

KING KONG was released by RKO Pictures on 7th April, 1933.

Credits:

Executive Producer	David O. Selznick
Directed by	Merian C. Cooper
	Ernest B. Schoedsack
Screenplay by	James Creelman
	Ruth Rose
Story by	Edgar Wallace
	Merian C. Cooper
Technical Director	Willis O'Brien
Director of Photography	Edward Linden
Musical Director	Max Steiner
Editor	Ted Cheesman

Cast:

Ann Darrow	Fay Wray
Carl Denham	Robert Armstrong
Jack Driscoll	Bruce Cabot
Englehorn	Frank Reicher
Weston	Sam Hardy
Native Chief	Noble Johnson
Second Mate	James Flavin
Witch King	Steve Clemento
Charlie (Cook)	Victor Wong
and	
King Kong	(The Eighth Wonder of the World)

To the opening bars of a lush thrilling score by Max Steiner, the name of King Kong himself concludes the cast credits. Then a legend, called 'An Old Arab Proverb' sets the theme of the film, and gives the audience something to ponder:

And the prophet said: And lo, the beast looked upon the face of beauty, and it stayed its hand from killing. And from that day, it was as one dead.

The film opens in the docks of New York during the great depression. A theatrical agent talks to a watchman about 'a moving picture ship' called the *Venture*, which has been chartered by an impresario, Carl Denham, for a 'crazy' voyage. The crew for the ship is large and the ship is full of explosives. Denham has not announced his destination nor his purpose, but he is making the voyage look like a military expedition. He is short of one vital element, a girl prepared to act for him. For he is filming a jungle hunt and he needs some love interest for his cameras. His reputation is for danger. What girl will go with him?

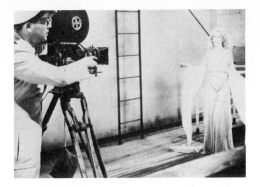

The night before the ship leaves, Denham goes out on the streets of New York to pick up his girl. He sees the hungry Ann Darrow trying to steal a piece of fruit. He rescues her and feeds her and convinces her to come on the voyage. She is a country girl, not 'one of these city gals who screams at a mouse and faints at a snake'. She signs on for the long voyage and the jungle picture.

The ship then sets sail under the orders of its tough mate, Jack Driscoll, who begins by inadvertently hitting Ann in the face. On the long voyage, Denham does some test shots of Ann, and he mentions the theme of his proposed film – *Beauty and the Beast*. He will not tell Driscoll where they are heading – he says he is no fortune-teller. But way west of Sumatra, he produces a chart that shows an unknown island, where the natives have built a huge wall to keep out something, 'neither beast nor man; monstrous, all-powerful, still living, still holding that island in the grip of deadly fear'. In case they meet the monster, Denham has brought with him a case of gas-bombs to stun it. Meanwhile, Ann must learn to pretend to scream!

42

A thick fog descends as the ship approaches an unknown shore. Through the fog, they hear the beating of native drums. The fog clears and they see ahead of them the island with a huge Skull Mountain rearing over it, and a vast wall separating the native village from the interior. Denham and Driscoll mount an armed expedition to get to the village, which they find deserted. The natives are all by a huge gate in the wall, shouting 'Kong! Kong!' A native girl kneels on an altar covered with flowers, while natives dressed as apes dance around her. Denham tries to get a camera shot of the heathen ceremony, but the natives see him and threaten to attack. A parley takes place between Denham and the native chief, who says the garlanded girl is the bride of Kong. He seems very interested in the blonde Ann, whom he calls 'the woman of

gold'. He wants her for Kong's gift, and he offers to buy her for six women. But, as Denham says, 'blondes are scarce round here'. So the Europeans beat a quick retreat back to the ship.

That night Ann and Driscoll play a tender scene on the moonlit deck. The woman-hater Driscoll tells Ann not to risk herself for Denham's ambition.

Ann: Why, Jack, you hate women.
Driscoll: Yeah, I know, but . . . you aren't women.

Driscoll has to leave the deck, and Ann is kidnapped by the natives, who steal up on the ship in their outrigger canoes. The drums sound loud from the island and fires burn. As Denham says, it looks like the night before an election. Driscoll discovers Ann is missing. All hands turn out and search the ship, only to find a native bracelet on the deck. Arming themselves with rifles and gas-

bombs, the crew sets out on a rescue expedition.

On the island, the natives open the huge gate and bind Ann to an altar outside the great wall. She is now the bride of Kong. They leave her tied as the sacrifice to the Beast and they close the great gate and cluster on the high wall, torches burning in their hands and drums beating. The chief chants for Kong to come and accept his sacrifice. A huge gong is beaten.

From the jungle, a growling is heard
and the crashing of trees. Ann screams
at the altar as the gigantic ape Kong
appears, his eyes glowing. His mouth
opens to show his teeth as large as
coffins. He watches Ann struggle and
scream on the altar.

Meanwhile, the rescue party from the
ship races through the village to attack.
Driscoll runs to a window in the great
doors, to see Kong lurch off into the
jungle with the screaming Ann in his
mammoth paw. Driscoll and Denham
get the sailors to open the great gate,
and with some of their men they pursue
Kong into the jungle. They follow the
broken branches and vast footprints of
Kong, until they meet a huge spike-
barbed reptile from prehistoric times.
Denham knocks out the Stegosaurus
with a gas-bomb, and the rescue party
moves on. The men reach a river and
make a raft to cross it. Another huge
reptile, a Plesiosaurus, attacks the raft
and destroys it, then begins eating the

A strip cartoon shows Driscoll stabbing at Kong's paw.

men, who try to get away. One man is gobbled up from the branches of a tree.

Denham, Driscoll and a few survivors escape only to encounter Kong, lurching along without Ann whom he has placed, like a white bird, high in a tree. Driscoll leads some men across a ravine on a fallen log, but Kong tears away the log and shakes the men loose. Driscoll survives by scrambling into a cave. Kong reaches over the ravine to fish for Driscoll with his paw, but Driscoll stabs at the giant paw with his knife. As Kong retires, another reptile tries to climb into the cave up a vine, but Driscoll severs the vine in the nick of time.

Ann is still perched in the fork of her tree. A gigantic prehistoric Tyrannosaurus Rex starts towards her. Kong hears her scream and battles with the Tyrannosaurus. The monsters grapple and gouge and roar, until Kong pounds the Tyrannosaurus, then prises its jaws apart before breaking them. He roars in triumph and picks up Ann again to

take her to his place.

Driscoll climbs out of the ravine to find that Denham is still surviving. Denham goes back to the main rescue party to get more gas-bombs, while Driscoll sets out after Kong. He follows the giant ape up to its cliff cave. Kong puts Ann on a ledge so she cannot escape, and leaves in search of food. But she screams, seeing a huge snake-like reptile behind her, and Kong turns to destroy the reptile, which tries to crush him to death. Again Kong roars his triumph and picks up Ann in his paw, then climbs high up the cliff where he settles down to examine Ann.

Kong lifts her in his paw, close to his huge eyes, and delicately tears off a strip of her skirt. She struggles and screams. Kong tears off a piece of her blouse. Ann struggles and screams. Kong tickles her, then puts her down with the last of her clothes still on her. He might have been pulling the wings off a moth.

Driscoll dislodges a rock behind him, as he climbs to the rescue. Kong leaves Ann to investigate. A giant pterodactyl swoops on Ann as its tidbit. It clutches her in its claws and flies off. Again Kong hears Ann screaming and grabs the vile bird out of the sky and pulls it down. The bird drops Ann, who crawls off to meet Driscoll. While Kong and the pterodactyl fight to the death, Ann and Driscoll escape down a vine at the side of the cliff. Kong kills the ptero-dactyl, and begins pulling up the vine. Ann and Driscoll let go their hold, fall into the water below, and escape.

At the village, Denham and the rest of the sailors wait. Ann and Driscoll make it to safety, but Kong is behind them. The sailors and the natives hold the gates, but the roaring Kong pounds them down. He towers over the wall and begins devouring the natives, also crushing them under his huge foot. He pursues the sailors to their boats. There Denham hurls the gas-bombs at him, and the mighty monster lurches and falls. Denham has him chained and floated out to the ship on a raft. The whole world will pay to see his prize. Kong will be controlled: 'He's always been King in his world, but we'll teach him fear'.

Dissolve back to a large theatre in New York, where there is an immense sign:

**King Kong
Eighth Wonder of the World**

A smart crowd packs the theatre, as Denham comes in front of a curtain to introduce his monster. The curtain rises and on the stage is the chained and crucified Kong. Ann is introduced as the bravest girl Denham has ever known. Kong begins to roar as he sees Ann, while Denham explains: 'There is the beast, and here is the beauty'. Kong strains at his chains as photographers blind him with flashbulbs. Then the chains snap on Kong's wrists. The audience screams and runs as Kong breaks loose and rampages out on to the streets of New York.

50

Ann and Driscoll escape and hide in a hotel. Kong looks for her, climbing up the side of the building. He reaches with his paw through a window to grab a girl asleep in her bed, and pulls her out. He sees it is the wrong girl and drops her indifferently down on the crowd below. He climbs high up the building and this time sees Ann and Driscoll in their room. He reaches inside, seizes Ann and climbs away to escape. Driscoll runs out to meet Denham, and they rush for the roof. There Kong roars his triumph, before making away with Ann across New York.

Another contemporary drawing shows Kong climbing the hotel, looking for Ann.

Kong now stands by the elevated railroad. As a train comes past, he swats it over the edge. Then he puts his mighty shoulder under the track and pulls the rails apart. Another train comes down the track and is wrecked in the gap. Kong pounds the train and crushes the passengers.

All resources are mobilised, as Kong begins to climb the Empire State Building with Ann in his paw. The police send for the airforce, while Driscoll pursues the giant ape to the pinnacled roof. Four biplanes with machine guns attack Kong on the spire

of the Empire State Building. They buzz round and round him like wasps, pumping him full of bullets. He swats at them vainly, only catching one and crushing it to pieces. Ann is put down on a ledge, but the wounded Kong picks her up again. He is hurt and dying, puzzled by the blood on his chest. So he puts Ann down again tenderly, then suddenly clutches his throat. He looks round, pained and pitiful. The fighters machine-gun him mercilessly, and he falls down the side of the tallest building in the world.

Driscoll rescues Ann from the ledge, while in the street, near the huge corpse of Kong, a police officer talks to Denham.

Officer: The airplanes got it.

Denham: Oh no, it wasn't the airplanes . . . it was beauty killed the beast.

KIN OF KONG

When the film of *King Kong* was complete, Merian Cooper advertised it by teasers. During the coming attractions in the cinema, a giant shadow would cross the screen and a voice would announce 'The Coming of Kong'. No more. Cooper's previous documentary had just been called *Chang*, which had meant 'Elephant'; he enjoyed tremendous monosyllabic names that hit the audience like a blow from a gong. For this reason, he rejected Edgar Wallace's original title, *King Ape*.

King Kong opened on the same night in the vast Roxy cinema and also in the new Radio City Music Hall. It was an instant and global success. And because it was a money-maker, Cooper, Schoedsack and O'Brien were sent back by the studio a year later to make a sequel, *Son of Kong*. As the father was meant to date from prehistory and had no mate, the son of Kong was smaller, more noble, more gentle, and much less successful. The scenario put Carl Denham once again on Skull Island to make his fortune – half of New York was suing him for the destruction caused by King Kong. This

The famous *King Kong* posters.

The poster of the sequel.
The white son of Kong playfully battles a prehistoric cave bear.

time the accompanying girl was Hilda, whose father ran a travelling circus. The party discovers an albino baby Kong, drowning in a quicksand. They rescue him and are rewarded by his heavy gratitude. He becomes the guide to the expedition, helps it to find a fabulous treasure of diamonds, and when an earthquake sends Skull Island below the sea, he holds up the Americans and the treasure on his paw until a rescue boat arrives. He himself is drowned, noble mammal that he is.

Song of Kong failed at the box-office, and although Cooper went on to make such triumphs as *Stagecoach* with John

Terry Moore poses by one of O'Brien's models for *Mighty Joe Young* . . . and his drawing shows the pet ape resisting capture by cowboys.

Ford, Willis O'Brien's talents were dissipated until he won an Academy Award for his third giant ape movie, *Mighty Joe Young*, again directed by Schoedsack. Made in 1949, the story was a saccharine version of the savage original. The starlet, Terry Moore, was made into the daughter of the owner of an African ranch. She has reared a vast black gorilla, Joe Young, from baby-

Mighty Joe Young behind bars.

56

hood. A promoter persuades her to do a night club act with her protégé. As she sings 'Beautiful Dreamer', sitting at a piano held in the air by the gorilla, a drunk makes him run amok, smashing the false safari setting of the night club to ruins and letting the lions loose from behind their glass cages. The police are about to gun the mighty ape down, but he rescues some orphans from a burning building. Thus he is spared to be put out to grass back on the ranch.

This sentimentalisation of the Kong legend by two of its creators was not matched by the other imitators of the film, who wished to get rich on the apparent craze for giant apes. Curt Siodmak made a film called *Bride of the Gorilla*, in which Boris Karloff was announced as the husband turned by a curse into a gorilla – Raymond Burr finally playing the bestial part. In the film, the terror of the girl facing the possibilities of a repulsive lover are

O'Brien's last giant ape supports his girl . . . meets the lions . . . and wrecks the night-club.

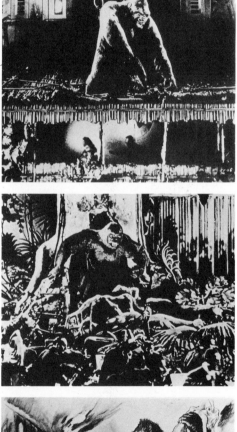

Mighty Joe Young
saves the orphans.

explored to the last scream and the ape's death, just in time. Sam Newfield's *The Jungle Woman* is even more explicit. A young girl, Julie London, is brought up like Rider Haggard's Hendrika by a giant ape – but to be his wife. In one scene, he battles with another ape for her charms. The film is worth little, although *Motion Picture Daily* claimed that it had 'the mystic elements and suspense of the Tarzan Stories'.

Left: Barbara Payton in the arms of the transformed husband in Curt Siodmak's *Bride of the Gorilla*. The pressbook poses usually hint at the profound possibilities of hairy rape.
Right: In an identical faint, Julie London is carried off by her gorilla guardian, Nabonga.

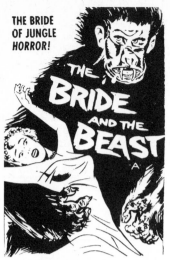

THE BRIDE
OF JUNGLE
HORROR!

The gorilla carries off his willing mate in *The Bride and the Beast*. Her screams are more pleasure now than pain.

Perhaps the most macabre version of the bride and the gorilla was an Allied Artists' shocker called *The Bride and the Beast*. In it, the wife of a big game hunter becomes 'strangely attracted' to the pet gorilla caged in her husband's cellar. The jealous husband shoots the gorilla, but his hypnotised wife has a dream in which she lives as a gorilla in a previous incarnation. Honeymooning in Africa, she is kidnapped by another

gorilla and taken off to live in a cave with a tribe of the beasts. Her husband tries to rescue her, but she chooses to remain with her ape mates. Civilisation loses. Bestiality triumphs. The woman gets her hairy demon lovers.

The possibility of woman-animal relations has, indeed, fascinated some film-makers, not only since *King Kong*, but also since the film made in the preceding year, *The Island of Lost Souls*. In it, a mad doctor, played by Charles Laughton, acts the role of Dr. Moreau from the novel by H. G. Wells. Laughton vivisects animals and men to make half-humans, half-beasts. In a famous line he declares, 'I took a gorilla and, working with infinite care, I made my first man'. Finally, his mutants destroy him, but not until his panther-like wife, played by Kathleen Burke, has been sacrificed to his jealousy. Similarly, Eric von Stroheim surrendered the lovely android, Hildegarde Neff, to a lustful ape in *Mad Doctor*. The experiment was greater than the attraction.

Yet the sexual tease of the gorilla and the blonde was never better exploited in a sophisticated way than by Marlene Dietrich in *Blonde Venus*. Joseph von Sternberg was far too clever a manipulator not to know the effect of a gorilla capering on to a night-club stage, removing its head, and revealing the billows of Marlene's hair, while she

H. G. WELLS'
ISLAND OF
LOST
SOULS
'X'

CHARLES LAUGHTON · LEILA HYAMS · RICHARD ARLEN · BELA LUGOSI *and* THE PANTHER WOMAN

The beast men from *The Island of Lost Souls* (1932).

strips her hairy skin to reveal her perfect body. The sequence was taken over, hair and hide and monkey, by Joel Grey in *Cabaret*; but even masquerading as a gorilla and a chorus girl, he could not excite us quite as much as Dietrich. Nor indeed could Aquanetta the Ape-Woman, the heroine of an extraordinary film of 1943, in which a beautiful girl is transformed into a gorilla. Somehow, *Captive Wild Woman* lost its sexuality in total absurdity.

1

3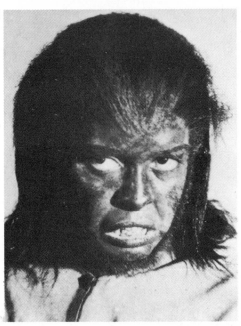

2

After the traditional mad scientist is menaced by his gorilla, Aquanetta is transformed into an ape in three easy stages in *Captive Wild Woman* (1943).

(1) The gorilla carries off Pamela Austin in the remake of *The Perils of Pauline* (1967).
(2) The lady explorer in *Tim Tyler's Revenge* (1937).
(3) The fearsome ape becomes a comic prop.
(4) W. C. Fields gets into a dilemma with a bottle of whiskey and a gorilla.
(5) This take-off of Kong treats the film as a children's lesson.

The ridicule of the mighty ape carried over into film cliché. In the serials, gorillas came on to carry off the woman in white so artificially that they might have been animated waxworks. And men in gorilla suits also ended up as stooges for stand-up comedians. The remake of *The Gorilla* in 1939 starred the Ritz Brothers with the mighty ape and Bela Lugosi. W. C. Fields could ignore the precedent, when he fell from an aeroplane in *Never Give a Sucker an Even Break* and found himself on a wall on the edge of a cliff with a gorilla – and a whisky bottle. The gorilla throws away the whisky bottle, and the anguished Fields escapes. What a waste!

LESSON 8.

This is the Empire State Building.
See the ape climb the Empire State Building.
The ape hates to ride elevators.
Hate, hate, hate.
Soon he will be attacked by planes.
They will be Spads.
and Fokkers.
They will be left over from old
World War I movies.
But his son will carry on with his work.
Being an ape is more exciting
than being an accountant.

It is the shame of a work of genius that it must be vulgarised and trivialised by its imitators. Comic strips endlessly used the ideas of *King Kong*, particularly the visions of the simian monster carrying away the sacrificial girl. In modern versions, the girl may even meet her fate – evidently better than death – and enjoy it as in the sophisticated *Phoebe Zeitgeist* under the dragon from Komodo. But in more primitive versions, the girls are rescued from modern simians by laser guns, while the good old uppercut still knocks out more traditional ape-men to save the nubile victim.

The *Beauty and the Beast* in Jean Cocteau's film of 1945.

Yet the epigraph of *King Kong*: 'It was beauty killed the beast', did help to inspire one version of the old fairy story of *Beauty and the Beast* which rivalled Kong in its lovely terrors and depth of emotion. Cocteau's film of 1945 made the Beast appear to be man, cat, and ape, and wholly sympathetic. Like Kong, he was a monster who loved his beauty in white; but he was human in size, wore the clothes of a prince, had the manners of a gentleman, and was transformed magically at the end of the film into the handsome Jean Marais, whose face had always slept beneath the hairy mask, and whose deep voice had spoken words of love from behind the fangs.

Cocteau's film, however, was too soon. The element of gentleness and fantasy in his man-beast was not required again for decades. Instead, a succession of shockers appeared after *King Kong* on the man-ape theme, exploiting the overt mass fears of murder and rape. The first group of these films gave pseudo-scientific reasons for the humanoid gorillas. In Paramount's *The Monster and the Girl*, the brain of a wronged man, executed for a murder that he did not commit, is transplanted into the skull of a giant ape. Using its new bestial strength, the brain begins murdering those responsible for the execution of its past human body. But while the pet dog of the executed man recognises its old master within the giant ape, the man's girl does not. So once again the Kong-like plot of the yearning ape and the screaming girl is reproduced, until the man-beast dies of bullet wounds, stretching out his arms to his unattainable love.

Dr. Renault's Secret, which depended on a similar plot of whether a murderer is man or ape, lost its suspense by showing the beast-man Noel swinging through the trees in human form. The doctor had managed to shave the hair off an ape, and to teach it to talk and act somewhat like a man. But this gift to popular evolutionary theory proved no gift to the doctor's neighbours nor to the cinema. Although sympathy for the man-ape is sought by his love of the doctor's fiancée, it is lost by the boredom of the action, in which J. Carrol Naish is about as frightening as Harpo Marx in a black wig. Yet even he makes a better job of primitive behaviour than the simian man in a film which Bela Lugosi might rather forget, *The Return of the Ape Man* (1943). This movie was a deception, anyway, since the equally inferior *The Ape Man* of the previous year had actually dressed the monster in a gorilla suit. In that film, Lugosi had played the lead, a scientist forced to murder people to get their spinal fluid, which he needed as an injection to stop

The man-beast looms sadly over his lost love, taken from a film poster of 1940.

The Ape Man looks as sad to be here as the audience was.

Another film poster of a man-ape, taken from a film of 1946.

Karloff appears in *The Ape* (1940), seeking spinal fluid.

of the Stevenson story made in 1931. In a later film, *The Split*, the schizoid nature of man and ape was even further explored. The scenario deals with a Japanese scientist, who experiments with enzymes which turn a newspaper reporter into a ravening gorilla. A second injection of enzymes leads to a climax on the edge of a volcano, where the monster reporter actually splits into two creatures, one the human being, the second the ape-like monster. The human manages to hurl his hairy half into the burning crater, before fainting and leaving the police with the insoluble problem – can

Fredric March as his evil self in *Dr. Jekyll and Mr. Hyde* (1932).

himself from becoming a gorilla. This, in its turn, was an imitation of the Karloff role in *The Ape* of 1940, where Karloff killed an escaped ape, and used its skin to ambush villagers. He also wanted their spinal fluid, but for a good cause – to prevent paralysis of all except the audience's critical faculties.

A better method of dealing with the simian in the human was the Jekyll and Hyde treatment. Frederick March, indeed, had won an award for his ape-like version of Mr. Hyde in the version

Man, ape and volcano meet in a thrilling climax to *The Split*.

The terror that split a man in two... half human half monster

THE SPLIT

CERT X

Starring PETER DYNELEY JANE HYLTON

with SATOSHI NAKAMURA · TERRI ZIMMERN · NORMAN VAN HAWLEY · TOYOKO TAKECHI · JERRY ITO
Original Story by GEORGE P. BREAKSTON · Screenplay by WALTER J. SHELDON · Assistant Producer ROBERT PERKINS   UNITED

Once again, the girl in white is menaced by a shape from our primitive past. In this case, she screams in the hands of *The Neanderthal Man*.

Greatest THRILLER-CHILLER Since "Frankenstein"!!!

HALF MAN...HALF BEAST...

THE NEANDERTHAL MAN'

STARRING

ROBERT SHAYNE · RICHARD CRANE
DORIS MERRICK · JOYCE TERRY

Directed by E. A. DUPONT · Written and Produced by AUBREY WISBERG and JACK POLLEXFEN
A WISBERG-POLLEXFEN PRODUCTION · PRESENTED BY GLOBAL PRODUCTIONS

UNITED
ARTISTS

Hairs and ape-like skulls even take over the make-up of *Frankenstein, Monster from Hell.*

Trog menaces a doll in this minute version of a theme from *King Kong* . . . and he rages in his cage like a gorilla.

a man be charged with the crimes committed by his worse self?

Where pseudo-science was not called in to create beast-men through transplants and enzymes, regressive techniques helped. *The Neanderthal Man* was created by reactivating the dormant memory cells in the human mind that harked back to primitive days in cave and jungle. The dream of ape showed on the face of the Neanderthal man. In the scenario, a mad doctor first sends the evolutionary spiral backwards by turning a pet cat into a sabre-toothed tiger, and then he experiments upon himself and becomes the Neanderthal man. After killing animals and human beings, he is torn apart by his own creation, the sabre-toothed tiger. The biter is bit, totally. Even Frankenstein's monster, himself, was given a treat-

ment in receding genes in one remake, *Frankenstein, Monster from Hell.* In this, Karloff's original sewn-up sadness goes ape.

Trog, on the other hand, is camp and gruesome, and it fails because it does not take itself seriously enough. Ape-men may be seen to be disbelieved, but they must be feared to be credited. Although Joan Crawford plays the anthropologist, who is certain that she has discovered the Missing Link in a cave and intends to educate him, even her fine acting and redoubtable screaming cannot save a silly film. At the end, the Trog actually hands back the girl he has kidnapped and allows himself to be dynamited. Yet he remains as unloveable as he is unbelievable, a figure of student fun, not of mass fantasy.

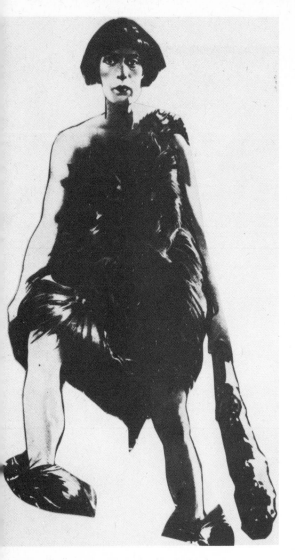

Buster Keaton menaces, in his way.

The kin of Kong were sometimes treated as his strict evolutionary heirs in the scale of history. On the principle that the world likes a circus as well as a monster, the escaping gorilla was a favourite theme of makers of shockers. In *Circus of Horrors*, for instance, death comes through knife-throwing and high

Raquel Welch is whisked away by an early bird.

Primitive man exults over his bloody trophy in *Creatures the World Forgot*.

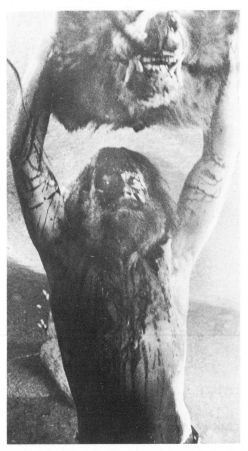

In a sense, the easiest way for providing blood-thrills from ape-man fantasies was to film the primitive men of prehistory and return to O'Brien's *The Lost World* and Bull Montana. In *Creatures the World Forgot*, for instance, the savage men can rape and behead as bestially as any ape running amok. And giant paws or claws can carry away a new favourite victim in white, Raquel Welch, who screams just as excitingly as Fay Wray. Time past can be an erotic past-time. Frankly, however, every Neanderthal man only serves to recall Buster Keaton's take-off of the genre in *Three Ages*, where the great stone-face makes all his successors absurd.

Ann Bancroft pays for her crime in a traditional embrace in the poster of the film . . . which, as usual, is rather more frightening than the reality.

LEONARD GOLDSTEIN
presents

GORILLA AT LARGE

A poster for *Konga* that promises more than it performs.

wires breaking, and mutilation is caused by plastic surgery; but the mighty gorilla still terrifies as he tears apart the bars of his cage. But in *Gorilla at Large*, where Lee J. Cobb and Lee Marvin find themselves trying to rescue Ann Bancroft from Goliath, the ferocious gorilla, the plot has a twist. It is Ann Bancroft who was a murderess previously herself in a gorilla suit, and although she is saved from Goliath, she is led away by the police to do her time.

But imitation, in the end, remains the sincerest form of flattery and the biggest box-office. Those films that built their ape dreams on the gigantic scale of Kong did better than their lesser rivals. The size of the beast does relate to the size of the budget. The British *Konga* of 1961 made great claims for itself. But it did not have the genius of O'Brien to animate it, only the vaunted Spectamation process of its producer, who had once wanted to call the picture, *I Was a Teenage Gorilla*. The great moment of the film is when a chimpanzee called Konga is injected with a plant serum from Africa, and grows to the size of a gorilla. Subject to the will of his paranoid creator, Dr. Decker, Konga strangles a rival and wrecks his laboratory. The doctor's wife, jealous of her husband's affair with a girl student, gives Konga another shot of serum to make him

Konga commits murder and mayhem on science.

Konga grows again, and the doctor's wife is terrified.

subject to her will. He then goes on the rampage, smashing up the doctor's laboratory, throwing the wife into the blaze, and breaking into a greenhouse, where the doctor's man-eating plants are just devouring the girl student. Seizing up his master in his paw, he lumbers off to Big Ben, where he is surrounded by the British Army and gunned to death. As he dies, he shrinks to the size of a chimpanzee again, and Big Ben strikes midnight, tolling the knell of an absurd film derived from a great original.

Konga lurches towards the hothouse ... and breaks in through the roof.

Konga dies by Big Ben, as he crushes his master.

Above and right: Godzilla burns up Tokyo with his fiery breath . . . and recoils as the pylons spit back electric fire at him.

Two Japanese remakes of *King Kong* were more amusing because of their simplicity and special effects, which at least were a pale copy of O'Brien's best. The Japanese had themselves invented a most successful screen monster, *Godzilla*, who destroyed Tokyo even more thoroughly than Kong had destroyed New York. Looking for a sequel, the Tokyo studio had the pleasant idea of teaming him up with King Kong. The result of twinning the monsters was that they could take buildings apart from both sides. Although Kong himself was

King Kong versus Godzilla, while a Japanese temple suffers between them.

presented in a highly simplistic fashion, the idea of making him stronger through electricity, and of floating him on balloons to his final encounter with Godzilla on Mount Fuji, had an inspired lunacy. This sequel was also successful, so that the Japanese now decided to introduce a robot giant. In *King Kong Escapes*, the primitive monster still battles primeval enemies and loves his blonde girl, but a Mechni-Kong has been created in a laboratory to free some atomic particles. The Mechni-Kong does not function too well, so the real Kong is again stunned by gas-bombs and floated back to Japan to get at the atomic particles. The radiation awakens the real Kong from his stupor, and he battles with the Mechni-Kong, who tries to kidnap his favourite blonde. In an epic fight on top of the Tokyo Tower (not quite as tall as the Empire State Building) the real Kong defeats his robot self, who burns to death on high tension wires and explodes when he falls to the ground. Kong then sinks the ship, carrying away the rest of his enemies, and turns back to his primitive bliss and domain, followed by the wise words: 'He's going home. He's had enough of civilisation'.

King Kong battles his robot replica.

So *King Kong* never dies, but lives for ever. Aptly, this last version of the legend reunites the main themes of the original with another chief thread of the fantasy cinema, the robot second-self, first popularised by Fritz Lang in *Metropolis*, when the mechanical version of Maria leads the workers to riot before being burned at the stake. The masters of modern industry, the Japanese, have fittingly grafted the mechanics of our time on to the Kong legend, leaving us with the question, not only of – is he man or ape? – but also – is he man or ape or machine? – which is merely a restatement of what we have always known to be true. Kong is really an animated machine anyway, projected by a dream machine that rouses our atavistic fears.

The mechanical Maria is made . . . and is tied as the false girl to the stake . . . and turns back to machine again. From Fritz Lang's *Metropolis* (1926).

APE DREAMS

The recent fashion for explaining human behaviour by comparing it with animal responses has set up the monkey as the moral teacher of man, as well as his demon. The works of Robert Ardrey and Konrad Lorentz on our innate and primitive aggressive behaviour have been followed by Desmond Morris in *The Naked Ape*, where he seeks to show that we are ape-like, indeed. These simian characteristics were explored in one of the more interesting films in the British new wave of the sixties, which pointed the way from the kitchen sink to the mental home, *Morgan – A Suitable Case for Treatment*. In the movie, our Kong-like fantasies of aggression are translated into an anarchic attack on capitalism. Darwin and Lenin walk paw in hand in this hilarious and under-rated film.

The hero, Morgan, is an artist, fond of flowers, children, Karl Marx and male gorillas. His trouble is that he acts out his fantasies. So he lays siege to his wife, who is trying to divorce him, putting a skeleton in her bed and cutting a hammer and sickle in her fireside rug. One day, he catches his wife in a gentle mood and they make love again, while the apes roar their triumph in the

jungles of Morgan's mind. But after this quiet interlude, Morgan's wife goes on with her plans for divorce, in order to remarry a wealthy art dealer. Morgan is distraught. 'If I'd been planted in the womb of a chimpanzee,' he says, 'none of this would have happened'. He goes to a wrestler friend,

David Warner in his gorilla suit on the rampage against the fickleness of his wife, played by Vanessa Redgrave.

Wally 'The Gorilla' Carver, to help him kidnap his wife and carry her off to the wilderness. She is furious and has him sent to prison. He reappears at her new wedding-reception in a gorilla suit, swinging in through the window and smashing up the gathering. His gorilla suit is set on fire, so he leaps on his motorcycle and drives into the River Thames. The ambulance men take him away in his sopping, charred hairy outfit, while he babbles happily: 'I've gone all furry'.

This remarkable film was the first to deal seriously with the fantasies of Kong. Morgan plays out the actions of Tarzan and the mighty ape. His rebellion against society and snobbishness is not just with words, but with the images and actions gleaned from fantasy jungle movies. The trouble is that, like the lesser imitations of King Kong in the cinema, Morgan himself cannot be the gargantuan ape, but only a lanky artist in a gorilla suit. His violence cannot match his imagination. And his final happiness can only lie in gardening in an asylum, knowing his ex-wife will bear his child – a far cry from his primitive reveries.

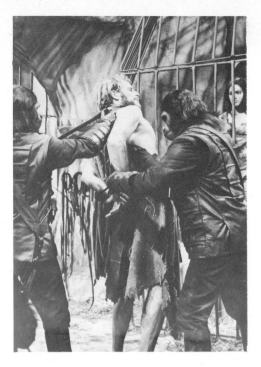

The film was, however, rooted in social reality, while the fantasy of ape-men needed to be Swiftian to make its moral point. When Pierre Boulle wrote *Planet of the Apes* in 1963, he took up the theme of Gulliver and the monkey in order to satirise our society, but in terms of science-fiction. In his version,

The apes prepare to round up their human victims ... and carry off Charlton Heston to the cage. From *Planet of the Apes*, the first of five successful films on this theme.

space travellers from Earth land on an unknown planet, where humans are no more developed than chimpanzees, while simians are as developed as humans. In a fearsome game drive, the humans are killed and netted by the apes for their scientific experiments. In Boulle's book, the human hero rapidly becomes adjusted to being treated as an interesting chimpanzee and to the sight of simians in clothes, doing Pavlovian tests. 'These monkeys, male and female, gorillas and chimpanzees, were not in any way *ridiculous*.' They never strike the hero 'as being animals in disguise, like the tame monkeys that are exhibited in our circuses'. They are the natural rulers of humans on their planet.

After a time, a female ape-scientist, Zira, manages to communicate with the hero, and delivers the logic of their thinking: 'Monkey is of course the only rational creature', she says, 'the only one possessing a mind at the same time as a body'. Man is a mere animal, only capable of mimicry. *Simius sapiens* evolved, while *homo* remained brutal. The reason was the use of four hands. It helped monkeys climb trees and understand the three dimensions of space, while men had to stay on their flat feet. Monkeys could use tools with far more dexterity than man. The ape is the mechanic, the human the pet.

The human hero, however, convinces Zira that he has come from Earth, and she is allowed to take him

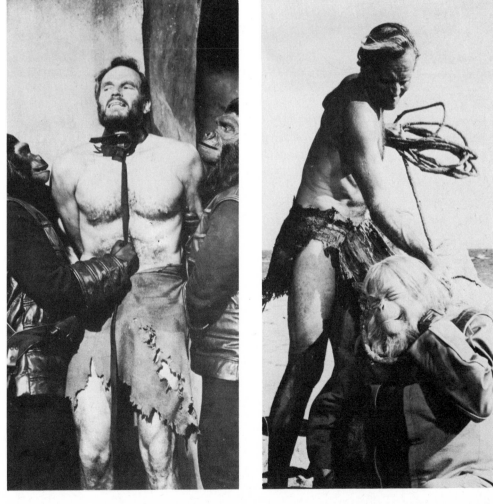

Charlton Heston on his leash with his ape guards . . . and getting his own back. He wears a loin cloth instead of being naked as in the original story.

out naked on a lead. He convinces the simian academy of sciences that he is as rational as they are, and he becomes the pet of monkey society. But he has his enemies among the old guard of ape biologists, and he has to flee for his life in his spacecraft with a wife and child picked up from the regressed humans on the planet of the apes. But on his return to Earth, he is met by gorillas, who have taken over his own planet in his absence.

Such is Boulle's novel. The brilliance of the first of the five films on the theme of the *Planet of the Apes* is to add a time warp. At the beginning, Charlton Heston, as the astronaut, discovers that his female companion in her time capsule has aged away recessively to a withered monkey. Man's simian origins

are hinted at, and when Charlton Heston is netted by the wise apes, he realises how their evolutionary process has outstripped man's on their planet. In Boulle's book, Zira and her lover, Cornelius, discover a ruined human city, which proves that human society originally ruled the planet before the apes took over and that the humans regressed to brutes. In the film, however, Charlton Heston, trying to escape across a desert, comes to the sea where a great ruined Statue of Liberty stands as lonely as the statue of Ozymandias. Heston looks at it and despairs. For he realises that his space-ship has gone in a circle through its time warp and he has landed on Earth again, *after* it has been taken over by the apes. He cannot escape. That is the end for man.

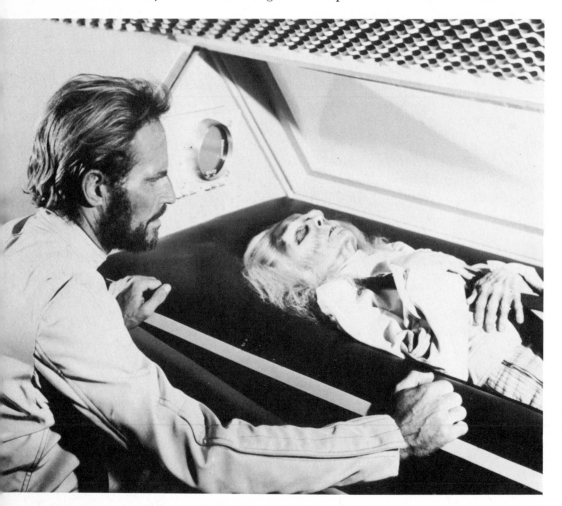

Something has gone wrong in the time capsule and the female astronaut has receded to a mummified ape.

Chimpanzees learning to be men, from *Zebra in the Kitchen*...
yet we still laugh at their effort and patronise them.

Yet it was not. The huge success of *Planet of the Apes* made 20th Century-Fox demand four sequels from screenwriter Paul Dehn. Dehn was ordered by the studio to destroy the whole planet and the cast at the end of the first sequel, and he dutifully did so, only to receive a cable six months later: 'Film great success. Further sequel required'. Dehn had to invent a son and a grandson for Zira and Cornelius, Caesar and Cornelius II. Dehn has always given credit to the inspiration of Boulle's original novel, writing that the fall of man and the rise of the primates becomes more and more true. 'The human race *is* declining. Apes are being taught to solve complex physical problems, to make reasoned choices, and to communicate with human beings.' The questions to Dehn are these: when will an ape's last grunt turn into his first word, or when will man's last word turn into his first grunt?

The four sequels carried the war between the wise apes and men to many reversals and conclusions. In *Beneath the Planet of the Apes*, the destruction of New York by atomic blast is seen. An astronaut sent off after Heston comes back to an underground civilisation of human mutants, who live in the cellars and subways of devastated Manhattan. They worship the cobalt bomb and have terrible powers in psychological warfare. Invaded by armed gorillas, they blow up the whole world in a solution worthy of Dr. Strangelove, and of a society that has learned to love the bomb.

In *Escape from the Planet of the Apes*, Cornelius and Zira and a third ape have rediscovered and repaired the original spacecraft, which first brought the astronauts to the ape-ruled planet. Thus they manage to get away just before the doomsday explosion, and they arrive back at the earlier human period in the history of the planet Earth. In their turn, they become curiosities in Hollywood, ape freaks in a freakish society. The pregnancy of Zira poses the dilemma that the rational apes may breed a race which will overcome men – and the apes are tried and condemned for it.

The final two sequels of the film series, *Conquest of the Planet of the Apes* and *Battle for the Planet of the Apes*, were both directed by J. Lee Thompson and resulted in fine fantasy films, although the budgets and the qualities of the scripts diminished. In the first of the two, the apes are enslaved by human society. Then they revolt and destroy the world in the atomic holocaust already described. In the final film, the few living beings left on the planet Earth are dominated again by the simians, wisely led by Caesar, the son of Zira and Cornelius. They exist in a tranquil Eden, but they journey to an atom-wasted city, where they find the race of human mutants. These mutants attack the apes, who are also threatened by a gorilla revolt within their own ranks. The apes, however, prevail and restore peace on earth and goodwill to all simians.

Paul Dehn gave three reasons for the success of the five films about the apes. They were top-notch science-fiction and attracted the children. They attacked what adolescents thought wrong about adult human society, and thus they drew in the students. And most curiously, black people went to see the films in large numbers, equating Ape Power with Black Power. Although any correspondence between apes and Africans might seem unfortunate, the victory of wise apes over degenerate white humans was seen as a triumph. *King Kong*, indeed, was taken as the title of the first black musical out of South Africa, which was successful there and in London. The theme of its mighty, triumphant, doomed gorilla (here played out in terms of a boxer) seemed apt to the black society of *apartheid*, questing and lunging after its rights.

Another mass appeal of the Apes films, particularly the last one, and of *King Kong*, lay in the concept of an escape to a simpler, more primitive Eden or garden, where might was not confused by right, where man could

The final battle at last, resulting in an ape victory.

THE FINAL CHAPTER

in the incredible Apes saga. The most unbelievable
showdown ever filmed as two civilizations battle
for the right to inherit what's left of the earth!

THE BIZARRE WORLD OF "PLANET OF THE APES" WAS ONLY THE BEGINNING...

Now civilization's final battle between man and ape is about to begin!

An ARTHUR P. JACOBS Production

BENEATH THE PLANET OF THE APES

The split between wise ape and human mutant.

The Dream, a painting by Henri Rousseau, called the Douanier. In it, the ape is tiny and distant in the trees and the lady naked and large in the foreground of our dreams.

express himself and be free. Once in the Lido in Paris, Zizi Jean-Maire made a spectacular comeback in a singing number, where she was raised from the stage floor in the mighty palm of a Kong-like paw. Behind her was a Douanier Rousseau set, all *naïf* and seductive. In that image of force and innocence, where the ape lived in his enchanted Eden, the nostalgic dream of Kong came true.

Yet the original *King Kong* still towers over all its imitators because of the power of its erotic nightmares. The series of films based on *The Planet of the Apes* have little strength in that respect – Pierre Boulle's account of the relationship between the astronaut and the bestial girl is far more sensual and Kong-like than the film version. For one thing, she is bare and unashamed throughout the novel; and secondly, she has the most perfect body that could be conceived on Earth. Her first appearance is spectacular, 'completely naked and without any ornament other than her hair' which hung down to her shoulders'. Moreover, she is in the cascade of a waterfall, 'standing upright, leaning forwards, her breasts thrust out towards us, her arms raised slightly backwards in the attitude of a diver taking off'. It is an entrance in literature worthy of Fay Wray's stripping in *King Kong*.

What Kong did was to establish an archetype of the abduction of the maiden in white. The hypnotised being in *Dr. Caligari* had set the style for the abduction of the sacrificial girl. But *King Kong* made the pose gargantuan and the eroticism both violent and horrific. The style of the Kong posters and of O'Brien's drawings became clichés in the work of his imitators.

Conrad Veidt abducts the victim in *Dr. Caligari*.

King Kong gets away with Fay
Wray.

Below and top right: The posters of the imitators of Kong show the
power of the image of the paw.

THE BRIDE
OF JUNGLE
ORROR!

THE
BRIDE AND **BEAST**
THE

Starring **LANCE FULLER · CHARLOTTE AUSTIN**

ALLIED ARTISTS PICTURE   DISTRIBUTED BY ASSOCIATED BRITISH-PATHE

Although the actual size of the brutes in *Bride of the Gorilla* and *The Bride and the Beast* was minute, the power of the hairy paw was monstrously emphasised on their posters. Even when an ape-like man played the monster, the hair and the nails of the hand were the terror. Moreover, Cocteau's beautiful version of *Beauty and the Beast* did not escape the archetype of the fantasy, female victim in the paws of the brute.

In *Phantom of the Rue Morgue*, the vile hand is larger than the victim – through fore-shortening.

CAN IT BE HUMAN?

"PHANTOM OF THE RUE MORGUE"

A human arm holds up the light as the Beast carries away the girl in Cocteau's film of 1945.

So Kong will triumph in the lusty labyrinths of the night. He was created in the 1930s, when film-makers still knew that the illicit should not be explicit—for films then had to pass more primitive censors. Not for the creators of Kong the vulgar assaults of modern monsters in comic strips. They knew of the power of Kong's puzzled gigantic size, of the nightmares created by his relentless pursuit, of the mass delight in his destruction of civilisation, and of the human pity given to his hopeless passion. We were once apes, we still behave sometimes like apes, and *King Kong* is the mightiest ape within us all. As Ralph Linton once wrote, we are, in fact, anthropoid apes, trying to live like termites, and not doing too well at it. King Kong is dead! Long live King Kong!

The Beast attacks the Beauty in a modern comic strip.

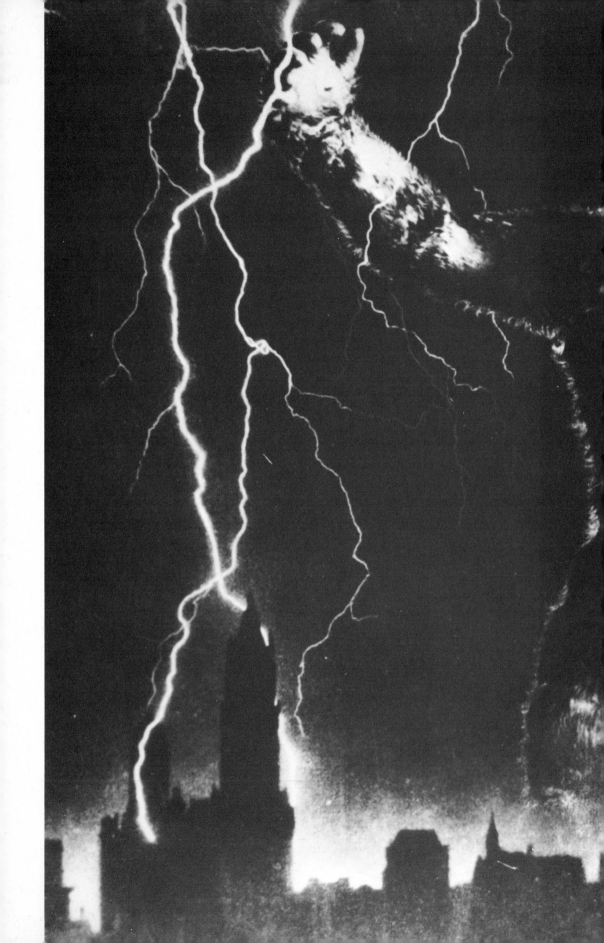

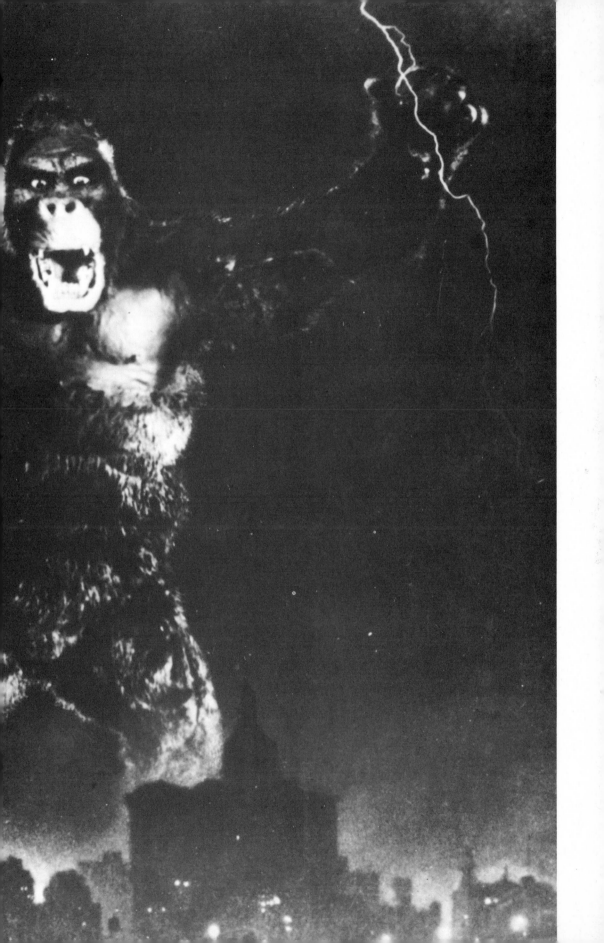